Praying
Next Generation

By Sally Michael

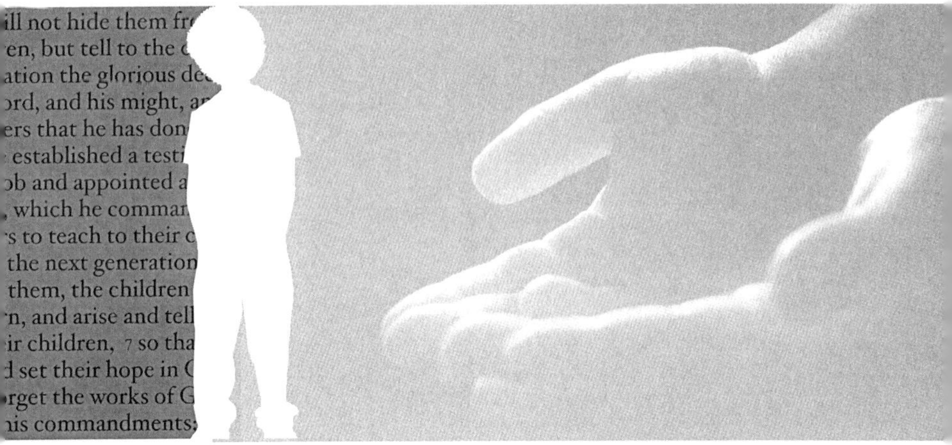

Truth:78

Praying for the Next Generation
by Sally Michael

Truth:78

1-877-400-1414
info@Truth78.org
Truth78.org

Table of Contents

The Legacy of Prayer

What kind of legacy do we want to leave for our children? Often as we get older and anticipate leaving this world, we diligently make plans for what we will be leaving behind. Some people label their possessions indicating who is to receive them after their death; others make strategic investments calculating how much they will leave to their heirs; most people draw up wills signed by witnesses; some get all their photos in order; and on and on it goes.

But how often have we thought through the spiritual inheritance we want to leave our children? Do we pray faithfully not only for them, but also for their children and our grandchildren's children? What better legacy can we leave than prayers prayed for future generations? What better "mark" can we leave as we pass from this life into the next?

In this world our children face a formidable foe. Satan *prowls around like a roaring lion looking for someone to devour* (1 Peter 5:8). One of our children's greatest defenses against Satan's attacks can be our prayers. Our world seeks to destroy the faith, moral integrity, and values of our children. Our prayers can be an effective safeguard and hedge around them.

Prayer is hard work—but it is also very rewarding. James 5:16b says, *The prayer of a righteous man is powerful and effective.* God has promised us great fruit from prayer, and yet we often neglect it. One reason that praying is hard is that we are easily distracted. For this reason, I have found it very helpful to pray with an open Bible. Many scripture passages can easily be turned into prayers. By turning key ideas in a passage into prayer topics, prayer can become both focused and very powerful. As we pray scripture, we discover God's heart as revealed in His Word and we can confidently pray for God's purposes.

This booklet has been written with the hope that you will not only faithfully pray for your children but also for the generations to come. It is intended to serve as a tool to help focus your prayers. The first section uses Psalm 1 to model praying through scripture. The second section includes 12 topics for prayer and some appropriate Bible passages for each topic. As you read the Bible, you may discover other passages that God lays on your heart for your children and their children. For this reason, some space has been left at the end of each topic for your own notes.

May God bless you as you strive for the faith of the next generations in your prayers,

Sally Michael

Psalm 1: A Prayer Guide

The Bible contains rich material for prayer. This section models how Psalm 1 could be used as a springboard for prayer. A sample paragraph follows each passage, demonstrating how each might be paraphrased in prayer.

Psalm 1:1—How blessed is the man who does not walk in the counsel of the wicked, nor stand in the path of sinners, nor sit in the seat of scoffers!

Don't let him listen to ungodly advice or follow the wisdom of this world; help him not to listen to the suggestions of evil men or be swept up into untruth. Don't let him follow ungodly friends or associate with those who despise the truth and sin against You; help him to choose good friends, and to love the people of God. Help him to love those who love Your Word and listen to the advice of those who would seek Your counsel. Don't ever let him mock the things of God or make fun of truth; help him not to be ashamed of the Gospel.

Psalm 1:2—But his delight is in the law of the Lord, and in His law he meditates day and night.

May he love Your Word; may the things of God be a delight to him. Help him to know the Word and to memorize the Word; may it be a ready defense for him in time of temptation or trial.

Psalm 1:3—He will be like a tree firmly planted by streams of water, which yields its fruit in its season, and its leaf does not wither; and in whatever he does, he prospers.

Make him strong in You. May he abide in You and bear much fruit. May he always prosper in the things of God. May he be full of truth and overflowing in love. May his life and character be marked with love, joy, peace, patience, kindness, goodness, faithfulness, gentleness, and self-control.

Psalm 1:4-5—The wicked are not so, but they are like chaff which the wind drives away. [5]Therefore the wicked will not stand in the judgment, nor sinners in the assembly of the righteous.

Unlike the wicked, may he stand strong in faith through all the storms of life. May he stand victorious to the end of his life so he can stand before You pure and blameless claiming the blood of Jesus, his Redeemer.

Psalm 1:6—For the LORD knows the way of the righteous, but the way of the wicked will perish.

Watch over his way all the days of his life. Thank You for being a faithful God and for working for Your children.

More Verses for Prayer

The following verses are easily converted into prayers for your children and form a core of key verses you'll pray over and over again. If you are new to using Scripture as a springboard for prayer, start with these verses. Then use them to supplement the scriptural topics for prayer in the following section.

Psalm 63:1-4—O God, You are my God; I shall seek You earnestly; my soul thirsts for You, my flesh yearns for You, in a dry and weary land where there is no water. [2]Thus I have seen You in the sanctuary, to see Your power and Your glory. [3]Because Your lovingkindness is better than life, my lips will praise You. [4]So I will bless You as long as I live; I will lift up my hands in Your name.

John 1:12-13—But as many as received Him, to them He gave the right to become children of God, even to those who believe in His name, [13]who were born, not of blood nor of the will of the flesh nor of the will of man, but of God.

John 15:5—"I am the vine, you are the branches; he who abides in Me and I in him, he bears much fruit, for apart from Me you can do nothing."

Psalm 119:10-11—With all my heart I have sought You; do not let me wander from Your commandments. [11]Your word I have treasured in my heart, that I may not sin against You.

Psalm 119:33-37—Teach me, O Lord, the way of Your statutes, and I shall observe it to the end. [34]Give me understanding, that I may observe Your law and keep it with all my heart. [35]Make me walk in the path of Your commandments, for I delight in it. [36]Incline my heart to Your testimonies and not to dishonest gain. [37]Turn away my eyes from looking at vanity, and revive me in Your ways.

Philippians 4:8—Finally, brethren, whatever is true, whatever is honorable, whatever is right, whatever is pure, whatever is lovely, whatever is of good repute, if there is any excellence and if anything worthy of praise, dwell on these things.

Colossians 3:1-2—Therefore if you have been raised up with Christ, keep seeking the things above, where Christ is, seated at the right hand of God. [2]Set your mind on the things above, not on the things that are on earth.

Proverbs 6:20-23—My son, observe the commandment of your father and do not forsake the teaching of your mother; [21]bind them continually on your heart; tie them around your neck. [22]When you walk about, they will guide you; when you sleep, they will watch over you; and when you awake, they will talk to you. [23]For the commandment is a lamp and the teaching is light; and reproofs for discipline are the way of life…

Proverbs 4:20-27—My son, give attention to my words; incline your ear to my sayings. [21]Do not let them depart from your sight; keep them in the midst of your heart. [22]For they are life to those who find them and health to all their body. [23]Watch over your heart with all diligence, for from it flow the springs of life. [24]Put away from you a deceitful mouth and put devious speech far from you. [25]Let your eyes look directly ahead and let your gaze be fixed straight in front of you. [26]Watch the path of your feet and all your ways will be established. [27]Do not turn to the right nor to the left; turn your foot from evil.

Additional Verses

____

____

____

____

____

Scriptural Topics for Prayer

This section lists 12 topics for prayer and suggests Bible texts for each one. There is a section at the end of each topic where you may record additional verses, insights you have while praying, or special requests and answers God lays on your heart. If you focus on one topic each month, you will pray through the entire list in a year.

1. ***Pray that they will trust Christ as Savior at a young age and treasure their inheritance as Sons of God. Pray that they will not accept Satan's design against them but walk in the light as heirs of the kingdom.***

   John 1:12-13—But as many as received Him, to them He gave the right to become children of God, even to those who believe in His name, [13]who were born, not of blood nor of the will of the flesh nor of the will of man, but of God.

   Psalm 63:1-4—O God, You are my God; I shall seek You earnestly; my soul thirsts for You, my flesh yearns for You, in a dry and weary land where there is no water. [2]Thus I have seen You in the sanctuary, to see Your power and Your glory. [3]Because Your lovingkindness is better than life, my lips will praise You. [4]So I will bless You as long as I live; I will lift up my hands in Your name.

   Hebrews 3:14-15—For we have become partakers of Christ, if we hold fast the beginning of our assurance firm until the end; [15]while it is said, "TODAY IF YOU HEAR HIS VOICE, DO NOT HARDEN YOUR HEARTS, AS WHEN THEY PROVOKED ME."

   1 Peter 2:9-10—But you are a chosen race, a royal priesthood, a holy nation, a people for God's own possession, so that you may proclaim the excellencies of Him who has called you out of darkness into His marvelous light; [10]for you once were not a people, but now you are the people of God; you had not received mercy, but now you have received mercy.

   1 Thessalonians 5:23-24—Now may the God of peace Himself sanctify you entirely; and may your spirit and soul and body be preserved complete, without blame at the coming of our Lord Jesus Christ. [24]Faithful is He who calls you, and He also will bring it to pass.

Galatians 5:1—It was for freedom that Christ set us free; therefore keep standing firm and do not be subject again to a yoke of slavery.

Additional Verses

____

____

____

____

____

____

____

____

____

____

2. Pray that they will hate sin and love godliness.

Romans 12:9—Let love be without hypocrisy. Abhor what is evil, cling to what is good.

Psalm 119:129-136—Your testimonies are wonderful; therefore my soul observes them. [130]The unfolding of Your words gives light; it gives understanding to the simple. [131]I opened my mouth wide and panted, for I longed for Your commandments. [132]Turn to me and be gracious to me, after Your manner with those who love Your name. [133]Establish my footsteps in Your word, and do not let any iniquity have dominion over me. [134]Redeem me from the oppression of man, that I may keep Your precepts. [135]Make Your face shine upon Your servant, and teach me Your statutes. [136]My eyes shed streams of water, because they do not keep Your law.

Ephesians 5:11—Do not participate in the unfruitful deeds of darkness, but instead even expose them.

1 Thessalonians 5:15—See that no one repays another with evil for evil, but always seek after that which is good for one another and for all people.

Philippians 4:8—Finally, brethren, whatever is true, whatever is honorable, whatever is right, whatever is pure, whatever is lovely, whatever is of good repute, if there is any excellence and if anything worthy of praise, dwell on these things.

1 Peter 5:8-9—Be of sober spirit, be on the alert. Your adversary, the devil, prowls about like a roaring lion, seeking someone to devour. [9]But resist him, firm in your faith, knowing that the same experiences of suffering are being accomplished by your brethren who are in the world.

3 John 1:11—Beloved, do not imitate what is evil, but what is good. The one who does good is of God; the one who does evil has not seen God.

Psalm 84:10—For a day in Your courts is better than a thousand outside. I would rather stand at the threshold of the house of my God than dwell in the tents of wickedness.

James 4:4-7—You adulteresses, do you not know that friendship with the world is hostility toward God? Therefore whoever wishes to be a friend of the world makes himself an enemy of God. [5]Or do you think that the Scripture speaks to no purpose: "He jealously desires the Spirit which He has made to dwell in us"? [6]But He gives a greater grace. Therefore it says, "GOD IS OPPOSED TO THE PROUD, BUT GIVES GRACE TOT HE HUMBLE."

7Submit therefore to God. Resist the devil and he will flee from you.

Matthew 10:28—"Do not fear those who kill the body, but are unable to kill the soul; but rather fear Him who is able to destroy both soul and body in hell."

Additional Verses

3. ***Pray that they will appreciate discipline and instruction, and be quick to repent. Pray that they will be caught when they sin. Pray that they will not be stubborn before the Lord.***

Proverbs 6:20-23—My son, observe the commandment of your father and do not forsake the teaching of your mother; [21]bind them continually on your heart; tie them around your neck. [22]When you walk about, they will guide you; when you sleep, they will watch over you; and when you awake, they will talk to you. [23]For the commandment is a lamp and the teaching is light; and reproofs for discipline are the way of life…

Hebrews 12:5-11—…and you have forgotten the exhortation which is addressed to you as sons, "MY SON, DO NOT REGARD LIGHTLY THE DISCIPLINE OF THE LORD, NOR FAINT WHEN YOU ARE REPROVED BY HIM; [6]FOR THOSE WHOM THE LORD LOVES HE DISCIPLINES, AND HE SCOURGES EVERY SON WHOM HE RECEIVES." [7]It is for discipline that you endure; God deals with you as with sons; for what son is there whom his father does not discipline? [8]But if you are without discipline, of which all have become partakers, then you are illegitimate children and not sons. [9]Furthermore, we had earthly fathers to discipline us, and we respected them; shall we not much rather be subject to the Father of spirits, and live? [10]For they disciplined us for a short time as seemed best to them, but He disciplines us for our good, that we may share His holiness. [11]All discipline for the moment seems not to be joyful, but sorrowful; yet to those who have been trained by it, afterwards it yields the peaceful fruit of righteousness.

Psalm 32:8-9—I will instruct you and teach you in the way which you should go; I will counsel you with my eye upon you. [9]Do not be as the horse or as the mule which have no understanding, whose trappings include bit and bridle to hold them in check, otherwise they will not come near to you.

Psalm 51:1-12—Be gracious to me, O God, according to Your lovingkindness; according to the greatness of Your compassion blot out my transgressions. [2]Wash me thoroughly from my iniquity and cleanse me from my sin. [3]For I know my transgressions, and my sin is ever before me. [4]Against You, You only, I have sinned and done what is evil in Your

sight, so that You are justified when You speak, and blame-
less when You judge. 5Behold, I was brought forth in iniquity,
and in sin my mother conceived me. 6Behold, You desire
truth in the innermost being, and in the hidden part You will
make me know wisdom. 7Purify me with hyssop, and I shall
be clean; wash me, and I shall be whiter than snow. 8Make
me to hear joy and gladness, let the bones which You have
broken rejoice. 9Hide Your face from my sins and blot out all
my iniquities. 10Create in me a clean heart, O God, and renew
a steadfast spirit within me. 11Do not cast me away from Your
presence and do not take Your Holy Spirit from me. 12Restore
to me the joy of Your salvation and sustain me with a willing
spirit.

Additional Verses

4. ***Pray that they will be protected from Satan and evil. Pray that they stand firm in persecution. Pray that they will be patient in affliction and look to God, trusting in His faithfulness when they have problems.***

   John 17:15—"I do not ask You to take them out of the world, but to keep them from the evil one."

   Romans 12:21—Do not be overcome by evil, but overcome evil with good.

   2 Corinthians 4:17-18—For momentary, light affliction is producing for us an eternal weight of glory far beyond all comparison, [18]while we look not at the things which are seen, but at the things which are not seen; for the things which are seen are temporal, but the things which are not seen are eternal.

   Psalm 121:1-8—I will lift up my eyes to the mountains; from where shall my help come? [2]My help comes from the LORD, who made heaven and earth. [3]He will not allow your foot to slip; He who keeps you will not slumber. [4]Behold, He who keeps Israel will neither slumber nor sleep. [5]The LORD is your keeper; the LORD is your shade on your right hand. [6]The sun will not smite you by day, nor the moon by night. [7]The LORD will protect you from all evil; He will keep your soul. [8]The LORD will guard your going out and your coming in from this time forth and forever.

Additional Verses

____

____

____

____

5. ***Pray that they will be responsible and loving in their relationships with others. Pray that they will walk in humility and look to the needs of others.***

1 Corinthians 13:4-7—Love is patient, love is kind and is not jealous; love does not brag and is not arrogant, [5]does not act unbecomingly; it does not seek its own, is not provoked, does not take into account a wrong suffered, [6]does not rejoice in unrighteousness, but rejoices with the truth; [7]bears all things, believes all things, hopes all things, endures all things.

Romans 12:9-21—Let love be without hypocrisy. Abhor what
is evil, cling to what is good. [10]Be devoted to one another
in brotherly love; give preference to one another in honor;
[11]not lagging behind in diligence, fervent in spirit, serving the
Lord; [12]rejoicing in hope, persevering in tribulation, devoted
to prayer, [13]contributing to the needs of the saints, practic-
ing hospitality. [14]Bless those who persecute you; bless and
curse not. [15]Rejoice with those who rejoice, and weep with
those who weep. [16]Be of the same mind toward one another;
do not be haughty in mind, but associate with the lowly. Do
not be wise in your own estimation. [17]Never pay back evil for
evil to anyone. Respect what is right in the sight of all men.
[18]If possible, so far as it depends on you, be at peace with all
men. [19]Never take your own revenge, beloved, but leave room
for the wrath of God, for it is written, "VENGEANCE IS MINE, I WILL
REPAY," says the Lord. [20]"BUT IF YOUR ENEMY IS HUNGRY, FEED HIM,

AND IF HE IS THIRSTY, GIVE HIM A DRINK; FOR IN SO DOING YOU WILL HEAP BURNING COALS UPON HIS HEAD." [21]Do not be overcome by evil, but overcome evil with good.

Romans 14:13—Therefore let us not judge one another anymore, but rather determine this—not to put an obstacle or a stumbling block in a brother's way.

Romans 15:1-2—Now we who are strong ought to bear the weaknesses of those without strength and not just please ourselves. [2]Each of us is to please his neighbor for his good, to his edification.

Galatians 6:1-2—Brethren, even if a man is caught in any trespass, you who are spiritual, restore such a one in a spirit of gentleness; each one looking to yourself, so that you too will not be tempted. [2]Bear one another's burdens, and thus fulfill the law of Christ.

Hebrews 12:14-15—Pursue peace with all men, and the sanctification without which no one will see the Lord. [15]See to it that no one comes short of the grace of God; that no root of bitterness springing up causes trouble, and by it may be defiled.

Ephesians 4:29-31—Let no unwholesome word proceed from your mouth, but only such a word as is good for edification according to the need of the moment, so that it will give grace to those who hear. [30]Do not grieve the Holy Spirit of God, by whom you were sealed for the day of redemption. [31]Let all bitterness and wrath and anger and clamor and slander be put away from you, along with all malice.

Philippians 2:3-4—Do nothing from selfishness or empty conceit, but with humility of mind regard one another as more important than yourselves; [4]do not merely look out for your own personal interests, but also for the interests of others.

Colossians 3:12-16—So, as those who have been chosen of God, holy and beloved, put on a heart of compassion, kindness, humility, gentleness and patience; [13]bearing with one another, and forgiving each other, whoever has a complaint against anyone; just as the Lord forgave you, so also should you. [14]Beyond all these things put on love, which is the perfect bond of unity. [15]Let the peace of Christ rule in your hearts, to which indeed you were called in one body; and be thankful. [16]Let the word of Christ richly dwell within you, with all wisdom teaching and admonishing one another with psalms and hymns and spiritual songs, singing with thankfulness in your hearts to God.

Colossians 4:6—Let your speech always be with grace, as though seasoned with salt, so that you will know how you should respond to each person.

1 Thessalonians 5:14-15—We urge you, brethren, admonish the unruly, encourage the fainthearted, help the weak, be patient with everyone. [15]See that no one repays another with evil for evil, but always seek after that which is good for one another and for all people.

Luke 6:27-28—"But I say to you who hear, love your enemies, do good to those who hate you, [28]bless those who curse you, pray for those who mistreat you."

Additional Verses

____

____

____

____

____

____

____

6. ***Pray that they will submit to God's lordship over them, and those He has placed in authority over them.***

1 Peter 2:13-17—Submit yourselves for the Lord's sake to every human institution, whether to a king as the one in authority, [14]or to governors as sent by him for the punishment of evildoers and the praise of those who do right. [15]For such is the will of God that by doing right you may silence the ignorance of foolish men. [16]Act as free men, and do not use your freedom as a covering for evil, but use it as bondslaves of God. [17]Honor all people, love the brotherhood, fear God, honor the king.

Romans 13:1-5—Every person is to be in subjection to the governing authorities. For there is no authority except from God, and those which exist are established by God. [2]Therefore whoever resists authority has opposed the ordinance of God; and they who have opposed will receive condemnation upon themselves. [3]For rulers are not a cause of fear for good behavior, but for evil. Do you want to have no fear of authority? Do what is good, and you will have praise from the same; [4]for it is a minister of God to you for good. But if you do what is evil, be afraid; for it does not bear the sword for nothing; for it is a minister of God, an avenger who brings wrath on the one who practices evil. [5]Therefore it is necessary to be in subjection, not only because of wrath, but also for conscience' sake.

Psalm 40:8—I delight to do Your will, O my God; your Law is within my heart.

1 Peter 5:6—Therefore humble yourselves under the mighty hand of God, that He may exalt you at the proper time...

Ephesians 6:1-3—Children, obey your parents in the Lord, for this is right. [2]HONOR YOUR FATHER AND MOTHER (which is the first commandment with a promise), [3]SO THAT IT MAY BE WELL WITH YOU, AND THAT YOU MAY LIVE LONG ON THE EARTH.

Additional Verses

7. ***Pray that they will choose godly influences. Pray that they would be led to good friends and away from bad friends. Pray that they would marry a godly mate.***

   Psalm 1:1-3—How blessed is the man who does not walk in the counsel of the wicked, nor stand in the path of sinners, nor sit in the seat of scoffers! [2]But his delight is in the law of the LORD, and in His law he meditates day and night. [3]He will be like a tree firmly planted by streams of water, which yields its fruit in its season, and its leaf does not wither; and in whatever he does, he prospers.

   Philippians 4:8—Finally, brethren, whatever is true, whatever is honorable, whatever is right, whatever is pure, whatever is lovely, whatever is of good repute, if there is any excellence and if anything worthy of praise, dwell on these things.

   Proverbs 1:10-15—My son, if sinners entice you, do not consent. [11]If they say, "Come with us, let us lie in wait for blood, let us ambush the innocent without cause; [12]let us swallow them alive like Sheol, even whole, as those who go down to the pit; [13]we will find all kinds of precious wealth, we will fill our houses with spoil; [14]throw in your lot with us, we shall all have one purse," [15]My son, do not walk in the way with them. Keep your feet from their path…

   2 Corinthians 6:14-18—Do not be bound together with unbelievers; for what partnership have righteousness and lawlessness, or what fellowship has light with darkness? [15]Or what harmony has Christ with Belial, or what has a believer in common with an unbeliever? [16]Or what agreement has the temple of God with idols? For we are the temple of the living God; just as God said, "I WILL DWELL IN THEM AND WALK AMONG THEM; AND I WILL BE THEIR GOD, AND THEY SHALL BE MY PEOPLE." [17]"Therefore, COME OUT FROM THEIR MIDST AND BE SEPARATE," says the Lord. "AND DO NOT TOUCH WHAT IS UNCLEAN; and I will welcome you. [18]And I will be a father to you, and you shall be sons and daughters to Me," says the Lord Almighty.

Hosea 2:6—Therefore, behold, I will hedge up her way with thorns, and I will build a wall against her, so that she cannot find her paths.

Proverbs 31:10-31—An excellent wife, who can find? For her
worth is far above jewels. 11The heart of her husband trusts
in her, and he will have no lack of gain. 12She does him good
and not evil all the days of her life. 13She looks for wool and
flax, and works with her hands in delight. 14She is like mer-
chant ships; she brings her food from afar. 15She rises also
while it is still night, and gives food to her household, and
portions to her maidens. 16She considers a field and buys it;
from her earnings she plants a vineyard. 17She girds herself
with strength, and makes her arms strong. 18She senses that
her gain is good; her lamp does not go out at night. 19She
stretches out her hands to the distaff, and her hands grasp
the spindle. 20She extends her hand to the poor, and she
stretches out her hands to the needy. 21She is not afraid of the
snow for her household, for all her household are clothed with
scarlet. 22She makes coverings for herself; her clothing is fine
linen and purple. 23Her husband is known in the gates, when
he sits among the elders of the land. 24She makes linen gar-
ments and sells them, and supplies belts to the tradesmen.
25Strength and dignity are her clothing, and she smiles at the
future. 26She opens her mouth in wisdom, and the teaching
of kindness is on her tongue. 27She looks well to the ways of
her household, and does not eat the bread of idleness. 28Her
children rise up and bless her; her husband also, and he
praises her, saying: 29"Many daughters have done nobly, but
you excel them all." 30Charm is deceitful and beauty is vain,
but a woman who fears the Lord, she shall be praised. 31Give
her the product of her hands, and let her works praise her in
the gates.

Additional Verses

8. ***Pray that they would desire inner beauty and godly character, and that they would grow more Christ-like daily. Pray that they and their future mate will be kept pure both before and after marriage.***

Ephesians 5:1-11—Therefore be imitators of God, as beloved children; [2]and walk in love, just as Christ also loved you, and gave Himself up for us, an offering and a sacrifice to God as a fragrant aroma. [3]But immorality or any impurity or greed must not even be named among you, as is proper among saints; [4]and there must be no filthiness and silly talk, or coarse jesting, which are not fitting, but rather giving of thanks. [5]For this you know with certainty, that no immoral or impure person or covetous man, who is an idolater, has an inheritance in the kingdom of Christ and God. [6]Let no one deceive you with empty words, for because of these things the wrath of God comes upon the sons of disobedience. [7]Therefore do not be partakers with them; [8]for you were formerly darkness, but now you are Light in the Lord; walk as children of Light [9](for the fruit of the Light consists in all goodness and righteousness and truth), [10]trying to learn what is pleasing to the Lord. [11]Do not participate in the unfruitful deeds of darkness, but instead even expose them.

Psalm 119:9—How can a young man keep his way pure? By keeping it according to Your word.

1 Timothy 2:9-10—Likewise, I want women to adorn themselves with proper clothing, modestly and discreetly, not with braided hair and gold or pearls or costly garments, [10]but rather by means of good works, as is proper for women making a claim to godliness.

1 Peter 3:3-4—Your adornment must not be merely external—braiding the hair, and wearing gold jewelry, or putting on dresses; [4]but let it be the hidden person of the heart, with the imperishable quality of a gentle and quiet spirit, which is precious in the sight of God.

1 Corinthians 6:18-20—Flee immorality. Every other sin that a man commits is outside the body, but the immoral man sins against his own body. [19]Or do you not know that your body is a temple of the Holy Spirit who is in you, whom you have from God, and that you are not your own? [20]For you have been bought with a price: therefore glorify God in your body.

Hebrews 13:4—Let marriage be held in honor among all, and the marriage bed is to be undefiled; for fornicators and adulterers God will judge.

Additional Verses

9. ***Pray that they will learn to walk in God's ways and actively resist Satan in all circumstances.***

Ephesians 6:10-17—Finally, be strong in the Lord, and in the strength of His might. [11]Put on the full armor of God, so that you will be able to stand firm against the schemes of the devil. [12]For our struggle is not against flesh and blood, but against the rulers, against the powers, against the world forces of this darkness, against the spiritual forces of wickedness in the heavenly places. [13]Therefore, take up the full armor of God, so that you will be able to resist in the evil day, and having done everything, to stand firm. [14]Stand firm therefore, HAVING GIRDED YOUR LOINS WITH TRUTH, [15]and HAVING PUT ON THE BREASTPLATE OF RIGHTEOUSNESS, and having shod YOUR FEET WITH THE PREPARATION OF THE GOSPEL OF PEACE; [16]in addition to all, taking up the shield of faith with which you will be able to extinguish all the flaming arrows of the evil one. [17]And take THE HELMET OF SALVATION, and the sword of the Spirit, which is the word of God.

Proverbs 3:5-7—Trust in the LORD with all your heart and do not lean on your own understanding. [6]In all your ways acknowledge Him, and He will make your paths straight. [7]Do not be wise in your own eyes; fear the LORD and turn away from evil.

Proverbs 4:20-27—My son give attention to my words; incline your ear to my sayings. [21]Do not let them depart from your sight; keep them in the midst of your heart. [22]For they are life to those who find them, and health to all their body. [23]Watch over your heart with all diligence, for from it flow the springs of life. [24]Put away from you a deceitful mouth and put devious speech far from you. [25]Let your eyes look directly ahead and let your gaze be fixed straight in front of you. [26]Watch the path of your feet, and all your ways will be established. [27]Do not turn to the right or to the left; turn your foot from evil.

1 Peter 5:6-10—Therefore humble yourselves under the mighty hand of God, that He may exalt you at the proper time, [7]casting all your anxiety on Him, because He cares for you. [8]Be of sober spirit, be on the alert. Your adversary, the devil, prowls about like a roaring lion, seeking someone to devour. [9]But resist him, firm in your faith, knowing that the same experiences of suffering are being accomplished by your brethren who are in the world. [10]After you have suffered for a little while, the God of all grace, who called you to His eternal glory in Christ, will Himself perfect, confirm, strengthen and establish you.

Psalm 143:10—Teach me to do Your will, for You are my God; let Your good Spirit lead me on level ground.

Psalm 86:11—Teach me Your way, O Lord; I will walk in Your truth; Unite my heart to fear Your name.

Additional Verses

10. Pray that they will be fully devoted to Jesus Christ and joyfully invested in the cause of the kingdom.

Romans 12:1-2—Therefore I urge you, brethren, by the mercies of God, to present your bodies a living and holy sacrifice, acceptable to God, which is your spiritual service of worship. [2]And do not be conformed to this world, but be transformed by the renewing of your mind, so that you may prove what the will of God is, that which is good and acceptable and perfect.

Psalm 119:10-11—With all my heart I have sought You; do not let me wander from Your commandments. [11]Your word I have treasured in my heart, that I may not sin against You.

1 Corinthians 15:58—Therefore, my beloved brethren, be steadfast, immovable, always abounding in the work of the Lord, knowing that your toil is not in vain in the Lord.

2 Corinthians 9:6-8—Now this I say, he who sows sparingly will also reap sparingly, and he who sows bountifully will also reap bountifully. [7]Each one must do just as he has purposed in his heart, not grudgingly or under compulsion; for God loves a cheerful giver. [8]And God is able to make all grace abound to you, so that always having all sufficiency in everything, you may have an abundance for every good deed.

Colossians 3:16-17—Let the word of Christ richly dwell within you, with all wisdom teaching and admonishing one another with psalms and hymns and spiritual songs, singing with thankfulness in your hearts to God. [17]Whatever you do in word or deed, do all in the name of the Lord Jesus, giving thanks through Him to God the Father.

Colossians 3:23—Whatever you do, do your work heartily, as for the Lord rather than for men...

Galatians 6:9-10—Let us not lose heart in doing good, for in due time we shall reap if we do not grow weary. [10]So then, while we have opportunity, let us do good to all people, and especially to those who are of the household of the faith.

Philippians 2:14-16—Do all things without grumbling or disputing; [15]so that you will prove yourselves to be blameless and innocent, children of God above reproach in the midst of a crooked and perverse generation, among whom you appear as lights in the world, [16]holding fast the word of life, so that in the day of Christ I will have reason to glory because I did not run in vain nor toil in vain.

Hebrews 12:1-2—Therefore, since we have so great a cloud of witnesses surrounding us, let us also lay aside every encumbrance, and the sin which so easily entangles us, and let us run with endurance the race that is set before us, [2]fixing our eyes on Jesus, the author and perfecter of faith, who for the joy set before Him endured the cross, despising the shame, and has sat down at the right hand of the throne of God.

Additional Verses

11. ***Pray that they would grow in faith and obedience, and in love for God. Pray that they would "not love the world nor the things in the world." Pray that that they would love the Lord with all their heart, mind, and soul. Pray that they would fear the Lord.***

Ephesians 3:14-19—For this reason I bow my knees before the Father, [15]from whom every family in heaven and on earth derives its name, [16]that He would grant you, according to the riches of His glory, to be strengthened with power through His Spirit in the inner man, [17]so that Christ may dwell in your hearts through faith; and that you, being rooted and grounded in love, [18]may be able to comprehend with all the saints what is the breadth and length and height and depth, [19]and to know the love of Christ which surpasses knowledge, that you may be filled up to all the fullness of God.

1 John 2:15-17—Do not love the world nor the things in the world. If anyone loves the world, the love of the Father is not in him. [16]For all that is in the world, the lust of the flesh and the lust of the eyes and the boastful pride of life, is not from the Father, but is from the world. [17]The world is passing away, and also its lusts; but the one who does the will of God lives forever.

Colossians 3:1-2—Therefore if you then have been raised up with Christ, keep seeking the things above, where Christ is, seated at the right hand of God. [2]Set your mind on the things above, not on the things that are on earth.

Matthew 6:19-21—"Do not store up for yourselves treasures on earth, where moth and rust destroy, and where thieves break in and steal. [20]But store up for yourselves treasures in heaven, where neither moth nor rust destroys, and where thieves do not break in or steal; [21]for where your treasure is, there your heart will be also."

Deuteronomy 10:12-13—"Now, Israel, what does the LORD your God require from you, but to fear the LORD your God, to walk in all His ways and love Him, and to serve the LORD your God with all your heart and with all your soul, [13]and to keep the LORD's commandments and His statutes which I am commanding you today for your good?"

Additional Verses

12. Pray that they would treasure God's Word and stand up for truth. Pray that they would be free from deception and the lies of the evil one, and have great understanding of the Word.

Psalm 119:33-37—Teach me, O LORD, the way of Your statutes, and I shall observe it to the end. [34]Give me understanding, that I may observe Your law and keep it with all my heart. [35]Make me walk in the path of Your commandments, for I delight in it. [36]Incline my heart to Your testimonies, and not to dishonest gain. [37]Turn away my eyes from looking at vanity, and revive me in Your ways.

Proverbs 2:1-5—My son, if you will receive my words and treasure my commandments within you, [2]make your ear attentive to wisdom, incline your heart to understanding; [3]for if you cry for discernment, lift your voice for understanding; [4]if you seek her as silver, and search for her as for hidden treasures; [5]then you will discern the fear of the LORD, and discover the knowledge of God.

Psalm 119:4-20—You have ordained Your precepts, that we should keep them diligently. [5]Oh that my ways may be established to keep Your statutes! [6]Then I shall not be ashamed when I look upon all Your commandments. [7]I shall give thanks to You with uprightness of heart, when I learn Your righteous judgments. [8]I shall keep Your statutes; do not forsake me utterly! [9]How can a young man keep his way pure? By keeping it according to Your word. [10]With all my heart I have sought You; do not let me wander from Your commandments. [11]Your word I have treasured in my heart, that I may not sin against You. [12]Blessed are You, O LORD; teach me Your statutes. [13]With my lips I have told of all the ordinances of Your mouth. [14]I have rejoiced in the way of Your testimonies, as much as in all riches. [15]I will meditate on Your precepts, and regard Your ways. [16]I shall delight in Your statutes; I shall not forget Your word. [17]Deal bountifully with Your servant, that I may live and keep Your word. [18]Open my eyes, that I may behold wonderful things from Your law. [19]I am a stranger in the earth; do not hide Your commandments from me. [20]My soul is crushed with longing after Your ordinances at all times.

James 1:5-8—But if any of you lacks wisdom, let him ask of God, who gives to all men generously and without reproach, and it will be given to him. [6]But he must ask in faith without any doubting, for the one who doubts is like the surf of the sea driven and tossed by the wind. [7]For that man ought not to expect that he will receive anything from the Lord, [8]being a double-minded man, unstable in all his ways.

Additional Verses

About Truth78

Truth78 is a vision-oriented ministry for the next generations. Our vision is that the next generations know, honor, and treasure God, setting their hope in Christ alone, so that they will live as faithful disciples for the glory of God.

Our mission is to nurture the faith of the next generations by equipping the church and home with resources and training that instruct the mind, engage the heart, and influence the will through proclaiming the whole counsel of God.

Values that undergird the development of our resources and training are that they be God-centered, Bible-saturated, Gospel-focused, Christ-exalting, Spirit-dependent, doctrinally grounded, and discipleship-oriented.

Resources and Training Materials

If you benefited from this booklet, we encourage you to consider other booklets for use in the church and home:

- *A Father's Guide to Blessing His Children*
- *Children in the Worship Service*
- *Discipleship Through Doctrinal Teaching and Catechism*
- *Helping Children to Understand the Gospel*
- *Mothers: Disciplers of the Next Generations*
- *Praying for the Next Generation*
- *Preparing Young People for Baptism: Pastor's Supplement*
- *Preparing Young People for Baptism: Mentor's Guide*
- *Utter Dependency on God Through Prayer*

Truth78 currently offers the following categories of resources and training materials to equip the church and home:

Curriculum

We publish materials designed for formal Bible instruction. The scope and sequence of these materials reflects our commitment to teach children and youth the whole counsel of God over the course of their education. Materials include curricula for Sunday School, Midweek Bible programs, Backyard Bible Clubs or Vacation Bible School, and Intergenerational studies. Most of these materials can easily be adapted for use in Christian schools and education in the home.

Vision-Casting and Training

We offer a wide variety of booklets, video and audio seminars, articles, and other practical training resources that highlight and further expound our vision, mission, and values, as well as our educational philosophy and methodology. Many of these resources are freely distributed through our website. These resources and training serve to assist ministry leaders, volunteers, and parents in implementing Truth78's vision and mission in their churches and homes.

Parenting and Family Discipleship

We have produced a variety of materials and training designed to help parents in their role in discipling their children. These include booklets, video presentations, family devotionals, children's books, articles, and other recommended resources. Furthermore, our curricula include Growing in Faith Together (GIFT) Pages to help parents apply what is taught in the classroom to their child's daily experience in order to nurture faith.

Bible Memory

Our Fighter Verses Bible memory program is designed to encourage the church, families, and individuals in the lifelong practice and love of Bible memory. The Fighter Verse program utilizes an easy-to-use Bible memory system with carefully chosen verses to help fight the fight of faith. There is a preschool version for younger children. We also offer a study and devotional guide that corresponds to the first year of Fighter Verses.

For more information on any of these resources contact:

Truth:78

www.Truth78.org
info@Truth78.org
Toll-Free: 1-877-400-1414

